The
Selected Poems
of
Isaac Rosenberg

Books by Jean Moorcroft Wilson

ISAAC ROSENBERG, POET AND PAINTER

I WAS AN ENGLISH POET: A CRITICAL BIOGRAPHY OF
SIR WILLIAM WATSON

VIRGINIA WOOLF, LIFE AND LONDON

CHARLES HAMILTON SORLEY, A BIOGRAPHY

SIEGFRIED SASSOON, THE MAKING OF A WAR POET

SIEGFRIED SASSOON, THE JOURNEY FROM THE TRENCHES

The
Selected Poems
of
Isaac Rosenberg

Edited and with an Introduction

by Jean Moorcroft Wilson

CECIL WOOLF · LONDON

First published in 2003
© 2003 Jean Moorcroft Wilson

Cecil Woolf Publishers, 1 Mornington Place, London NW1 7RP
Tel: 020 7387 2394

British Library Cataloguing-in-Publication Data
A catalogue record of this book is available from the British Library

ISBN 1-897967-38-1

Front cover: Self-portrait by Isaac Rosenberg,
oil on canvas, *c.* 1914

Contents

Introduction

Isaac Rosenberg, one of the finest of the First World War poets, is also one of its most distinctive. Differing widely in terms of race, class, upbringing and experience from almost all the other well-known names of the period, he brings to his work a fierce originality of both vision and technique which makes him not always the most accessible of them. This helps to explain his much slower rise to fame than Brooke, Sassoon or Owen, for example. While Rosenberg's contemporaries, including the half-Jewish Siegfried Sassoon, drew largely on the Christian and classical mythology they had absorbed through their traditional English education, Rosenberg was influenced by a different cultural heritage. As Sassoon himself puts it in his foreword to Rosenberg's *Collected Works* of 1937, his work shows 'a fruitful fusion between English and Hebrew culture'. Behind all his poetry, Sassoon argues, 'there is a racial quality – biblical and prophetic. Scriptural and sculptural...'[1]

* * * *

Rosenberg's parents, Anna and Barnett, arrived in Bristol with their daughter Minnie in the late 1880s, having emigrated originally from Devinsk in Lithuania to escape increasingly savage anti-Semitic laws and pogroms. Though a cultured man, who himself wrote poetry, Barnett Rosenberg took up work as a peddler, a trade he considered socially beneath him but one which allowed him to maintain a certain amount of independance. The family settled down in one of Bristol's slums and it was there, at 5 Adelaide Place, that their first son and second child, Isaac, was born on 25 November 1890. But before he was seven years old, his parents had decided to move on again to London, a decision based partly on their determination to give Isaac a sound Jewish education.

Gravitating naturally towards the East End of London, where many other Jewish refugees had congregated, the family found lodgings at 47 Cable Street, Stepney, where they lived, now seven in all, in one room, later moving to a small house of their own at Jubilee Street in the same deprived area. The house was overcrowded but had also to be let out in part to help pay the rent and feed and clothe their six children, who were educated at indifferent state schools. It was an existence on the edge of destitution and would remain so for most of Isaac's childhood and teenage years. It is against this background of severely limited horizons that we must measure his achievements. For his poverty, as much as his Jewishness, marked his life and shaped his work, as he himself would point out.

As a very young child Rosenberg had wanted to be an artist as well as a poet, but family circumstances dictated that he had to leave school at fourteen and take a job. Trying to cater to his artistic interests, his mother found him an apprenticeship with an engraver, like William Blake, whom Rosenberg also resembled in his dedication to both art and poetry. Unlike Blake, however, Rosenberg found engraving tedious. After two years as an apprentice engraver he took up night classes in art at Birkbeck College and won several prizes between 1907 and 1909, but he longed to study the subject full-time.

8

His sense of frustration emerges very clearly in a letter written to a sympathetic friend in 1910:

> It is horrible to think that all these hours, when my days are full of vigour and my hands and soul craving for self-expression, I am bound, chained to this fiendish mangling-machine, without hope and almost desire of deliverance, and the days of youth go by... I have tried to make some sort of self-adjustment to circumstances by saying, 'It is all *experience*'; but, good God! it is *all* experience, and nothing else.[2]

Though Rosenberg had also started writing poetry seriously by the time he wrote this letter, there is no doubt that art came first for him. Whilst he felt he might 'do something' in art, he told the same friend: 'I despair of ever writing excellent poetry. I can't look at things in the simple, large way that great poets do. My mind is so cramped and dulled and fevered, there is no consistency of purpose, no oneness of aim; the very fibres are torn apart, and application deadened by the fiendish persistence of the coil of circumstance'.[3] And though he would eventually receive a first-class training in art, he was never formally prepared for his writing of poetry, a lack he felt acutely. Writing to Miss Seaton, who attempted to remedy the situation, he reminded her:

> You mustn't forget the circumstances I have been brought up in, the little education I have had. Nobody ever told me what to read, or ever put poetry in my way. I don't think I knew what real poetry was till I

read Keats a couple of years ago. True, I galloped through Byron when I was about fourteen, but I fancy I read him more for the story than the poetry. I used to try to imitate him. Anyway, if I didn't quite take to Donne at first, you understand why. Poetical appreciation is only newly bursting on me.[4]

It could be argued that it is precisely this absence of formal preparation which helps to account for the striking originality of Rosenberg's verse, as well as its technical unevenness.

Rosenberg's attempts to make up for his lack of literary background were almost certainly the result of his meeting at the age of twenty with three young men who, like himself, aspired to be writers or painters, Joseph Leftwich, Stephen Winsten and John Rodker. Together with Rosenberg, and later Mark Gertler and David Bomberg, they came to be known as 'The Whitechapel Boys'. 'We were the slum children, the problem youth, the beneficiaries of the Board of Guardians and the soup kitchen, and some of us (like Rosenberg and Bomberg) of the Jewish Educational Aid Society', wrote Leftwich, who himself went on to become a writer. Coming mainly from overcrowded and deprived homes, their meeting-places were Whitechapel's Public Library and Art Gallery, which also provided them with the means of further education.

Rosenberg's membership of the Whitechapel Group undoubtedly strengthened his resolve to become either a painter or poet and in 1911 he threw in his job as an engraver. With no clear sense of direction or any visible means of support, he was very fortunate indeed to be taken up by three wealthy Jewish ladies, Mrs Delissa Joseph, Mrs Henrietta Lōwy and Mrs Herbert Cohen, who offered to pay his fees at the Slade School of Art. He studied there between 1911 and 1914, taught by such well-known figures as Tonks, Brown, Steer and MacEvoy, and surrounded by students who were themselves to become famous in the history of twentieth-century art — Mark Gertler, David Bomberg, Edward Wadsworth, Charles Nevinson, Paul Nash, Dora Carrington and Stanley Spencer. Though Rosenberg was never to become well-known as a painter, he did win at least one prize during his three years at the Slade, also selling work to the New English Art Club and exhibiting several pictures at the Imperial Institute Galleries in South Kensington.

Meantime, in spite of self-doubts, Rosenberg was continuing with his poetry. In 1912 he wrote to Laurence Binyon for advice and in 1913 was introduced to Edward Marsh, a generous patron of young poets and painters. Besides buying his pictures and encouraging him to write, Marsh also introduced Rosenberg to some of his many friends, among them one of the most controversial thinkers of the period, T.E. Hulme. It was through Hulme that Rosenberg met Ezra Pound, then at the height of his Imagist phase. Unhampered by Marsh's traditional expectations of verse, Pound liked Rosenberg's work sufficiently to send some of it to Harriet Monroe, editor of the influential *Poetry* magazine in Chicago. 'I think you may as well give the poor devil a show', he wrote to her laconically, adding: 'He has something in him, horribly rough but then "Stepney, East" ... we ought to have a real...burglar, ma che!!!'. In spite of the somewhat patronizing nature of Pound's recommendation, Monroe would eventually print several of Rosenberg's poems, giving a much-needed boost to his frail self-confidence.

By the time Rosenberg's poems were published in *Poetry* in 1916, he had already published two pamphlets at his own expense, *Night and Day* (1912) and *Youth* (1915). The second of these had been funded by the sale of three paintings to Marsh, but long before it appeared in April 1915 Rosenberg had realized that he would be unable to earn his living by either his poetry or his painting and had gone to stay with his eldest sister, Minnie, in South Africa. He was just settling down there when war broke out in Europe in August 1914. Showing no inclination to return home, though he did write a poem on the occasion, 'On Receiving News of the War', he continued his efforts to establish himself in Cape Town. When neither his painting nor writing, nor even lecturing on art seemed any more likely to succeed there than in England, he decided to return home. His decision was certainly not prompted by patriotism, since he had no desire to, nor intention of fighting for his country.

When Rosenberg did finally enlist towards the end of 1915, he was entirely frank about his motives: 'I never joined the army for patriotic reasons,' he wrote to Marsh from his training depot. 'Nothing can justify war. I suppose we must all fight to get the trouble over'.[5] Another incentive, he admitted, had been money: 'I thought if I'd join there would be the separation allowance for my mother'.[6] For, as he told another of his patrons, Sydney Schiff, he had been unable to get work elsewhere.

At least if he had to join the Army, he decided, he would apply for the Royal Army Medical Corps, but his diminutive stature disqualified him from anything but the Bantam units, formed by 1915 in an attempt to remedy the acute shortage of men. Posted to the Bantam Battalion of the 12th Suffolk Regiment in October 1915, he was quickly transferred, first to the 12th South Lancashires in January 1916, then finally to the 11th King's Own Royal Lancasters in March 1916. By July 1916 he was out in France with them, but kept behind the lines at the 40th Division Salvage Office. Reassigned to the 40th Division Works Battalion in February 1917 and later the same month to the 229th Field Company of the Royal Engineers, attached to the 11th King's Own Royal Lancasters, he led an unsettled, deeply unhappy existence. A poor soldier, he experienced little but criticism and punishment. In February 1918, he was transferred yet again, this time to the 1st King's Own Royal Lancasters, and recalled to the trenches in March. A month later he was dead. In the great German offensive of 1918, the main attack was launched against the British Third and Fifth Armies and as part of the Third Army Rosenberg's battalion had been brought into the front line by 21 March. For three days they helped ward off the enemy, then were sent back into reserve. Two days later the Germans broke through to capture land they had not occupied since 1914. During the ensuing battle Rosenberg was killed on patrol by a German raiding-party at dawn on April Fool's Day, 1918.

His end was not a glorious one, but it was distinguished by a certain pathos. For in a letter to Marsh four days before his death he had written: 'It's really my being lucky enough to bag an inch of candle that incites me to this pitch of punctual epistolary. I must measure my letter by the light'. By the time Marsh received the letter on 2 April 1918, Rosenberg's own light had gone out.

Isaac Rosenberg's insignificant military career and unlucky end was sadly all too common in the First World War and would not be of any special interest, had he not emerged as one of the most powerful poets of that war. As it is, his attitude towards the conflict into which he had been so unwillingly drawn is of prime importance to an understanding of his work.

His initial response to the war in 1914 had been a fairly conventional one, as a poem like 'The Dead Heroes' (see page 38) shows. But his attitude gradually hardened, becoming harsher and more realistic, particularly after he reached the trenches. He was critical of Rupert Brooke's 'begloried sonnets',[7] which seemed to him 'commonplace', finding their romantic lyricism inappropriate to the ugliness and horror he encountered in wartime France. Like Owen, Sassoon, Sorley and Graves, among others, he judged the old reactions and techniques inadequate.

Unlike those officer poets, however, Rosenberg saw war from a private soldier's point of view. Though not unique in this, it does give his work an unusual angle which helps to distinguish it from the bulk of First World War poetry. In 'Marching' (p. 39), for instance, he describes the men as one of them and in 'Break of Day in the Trenches' (pp. 42-43) he identifies with the lowly rat against the 'haughty athletes'.

Being a private meant that Rosenberg led a harder life

in the line than the officer-poets while not having to suffer their strong sense of responsibility and, in Sassoon's case at least, guilt. He was also less privileged in terms of leave; he served almost twenty months in or near the trenches with only two brief respites. For him war became an everyday experience of such rigour that he had little time to theorise about it, much less beautify it. Such conditions may also help to explain why Rosenberg's work often has a more visceral quality than that of the officer-poets: wheels 'lurch[ing] over sprawled dead' as their 'bones crunched' and 'a man's brains splatter[ing] on / A stretcher-bearer's face' in 'Dead Man's Dump' clearly come from first-hand experience.

It is not surprising that Rosenberg hated Army life. Being an incompetent soldier, much too untidy and absent-minded to satisfy his superiors, he was constantly in trouble and he found the physical hardships almost unbearable. Yet, ironically, it was in such circumstances that he produced his finest work. He had written to Laurence Binyon in 1916: 'I will not leave a corner of my consciousness covered up, but saturate myself with the strange and extraordinary new conditions of this life, and it will all refine itself into poetry later on'.[8] And his determination 'that this war, with all its powers for devastation, shall not master my poeting' had triumphed.[9] Though his war-poetry represents only about one-tenth of his work as a whole, it has deservedly established his reputation and drawn attention to his earlier but no less interesting work.

*   *   *   *

The poetry of Isaac Rosenberg raises certain questions, one of the most difficult to answer being the effect his

15

poverty had on his work. Rosenberg himself had strong views on the matter: 'When one has to think of responsibilities, when one has to think strenuously how to manage to subsist, so much thought, so much energy is necessarily taken from creative work', he wrote in his autobiographical story 'Rudolph'. 'It might widen experience and develop a precocious mental maturity, of thought and worldliness, it might even make one's work more poignant and intense, but I am sure the final result is loss, technical incompleteness, morbidity and the evidence of tumult and conflict'.[10] This may be true in Rosenberg's own case, though it could equally well be that his own attitude produced many of the symptoms he mentions. Poverty does not inevitably diminish creative energy. In the case of Rosenberg's friend Mark Gertler, for instance, it seems to have produced a challenge which stimulated him to greater effort. But Rosenberg appears to have started life with less energy and to have been more deeply affected by his deprived upbringing, of which he never lost sight.

His attitude towards his Jewishness is more difficult to define. Born into an orthodox family, he was given a traditional Jewish education as well as an English one. As a child he was 'fervently religious' and his first extant poems, 'David's Harp' and 'Zion', are specifically Jewish in theme. His enthusiasm and orthodoxy decreased as he matured, however, and this too is reflected in his work. None of the poems in the booklet *Night and Day* of 1912 is overtly Jewish and its one religious piece, 'Spiritual Isolation', beside suggesting a sense of spiritual barrenness, describes a God of no defined faith:

16

My Maker shunneth me:
Even as a wretch stricken with leprosy,
So hold I pestilent supremacy.
Yea! He hath fled as far as the uttermost star,
Beyond the unperturbed fastnesses of night
And dreams that bastioned are
By fretted towers of sleep that scare His light.

(p. 65)

Jon Silkin sees this poem as an expression of the root-lessness of Jewry in the alien, if not partly hostile, English community, and emphasises the importance of the image of rootlessness in Rosenberg's poetry, partic-ularly in 'Chagrin' (see p. 77).

Silkin recognises, however, that Rosenberg finally rejected a 'passive attitude to Fate' and argues that in doing so he 'broke with the traditional role of Jewish victim (though maintaining a stoic attitude to Fate) as well as with a society whose upper class imposed on its poor those economic and cultural taxes which kept its position intact'. Rosenberg was certainly not regarded as intensely religious by friends who knew him between 1910 and 1912. While most of the Whitechapel group were still involved with orthodox Judaism and some were keen Zionists, Rosenberg seemed to them to have no religious commitments. His attitude to Jewishness at that time is expressed most clearly in his review, 'Romance at the Baillie Galleries: the Works of J.H. Amschewitz and the late H. Ospovat'. Having argued that one would not suspect these artists of being Jewish, he continues:

Whether this is something to be deplored or not is

beside the question here, as it is the inevitable result of ages of assimilation and its blame (if a defect) is to be placed on the causes that made us a race, and unmade us as a nation. Yet though these causes have deprived us of any exclusive atmosphere such as our literature possesses, they have given that which nothing else could have given. The travail and sorrow of centuries have given life a more poignant and intense interpretation, while the strength of the desire of ages has fashioned an ideal which colours all our expression of existence.[11]

By 1913 Rosenberg was openly rejecting orthodoxy:

> Moses must die to live in Christ,
> The seed be buried to live to green.
> Perfection must begin from worst.
> Christ perceives a larger reachless love,
> More full, and grows to reach thereof.
>
> ('Creation')

This is one of very few poems in which Rosenberg refers directly to Christianity. On the whole his religious position is ambiguous enough to admit of various interpretations. Joseph Cohen, for instance, argues that Rosenberg 'rejected Judaism's fundamental tenet, the belief in a patriarchal deity, in favour of a Pre-Hebraic matriarchal mythology.... In any case he was not orthodox'.[12]

For all that, however, Rosenberg still thought in terms of a masculine deity as late as 1916. He does not seem to have worked out any coherent philosophy before his death. One thing alone is certain — that Rosenberg felt increasingly rebellious towards the only God he could believe in. Two poems in his 1915 collection — 'The One Lost' and 'God Made Blind' — suggest that he took pleasure in the idea of outwitting a deity who seems to him malign as well as beneficent. This attitude is spelt out in 'God', published in *Moses* in 1916:

In his malodorous brain what slugs and mire,
Lanthorned in his oblique eyes, guttering burned!
His body lodged a rat where men nursed souls.
The world flashed grape-green eyes of a foiled cat
To him. On fragments of an old shrunk power,
On shy and maimed, on women wrung awry,
He lay, a bullying hulk, to crush them more.
But when one, fearless, turned and clawed
   like bronze,
Cringing was easy to blunt these stern paws,
And he would weigh the heavier on those after.
      *   *   *   *
Ah! this miasma of a rotting God!

Rosenberg's hostility towards God was almost certainly intensified by the conditions of the war in which he was personally involved by late 1915. Yet at the same time it seems to have revived his interest in Judaism, as his army poems show. Apart from his published dramatic poem about the Jewish hero, Moses, he started a second, 'The Unicorn', centred round another famous Hebrew, Saul, though it is not exclusively Jewish. He planned yet a third play, he told Laurence Binyon in 1916, 'round our Jewish hero, Judas Maccabeus', since he felt there was 'some parallel in the savagery of the invaders then to this war'.[13] And shortly before his death he confided to his brother, Dave, 'I wanted to write a battle song for the Judaens but so far I can think of nothing noble and weighty enough'.[14] Beside planning Jewish poems, he actually produced four in the trenches. The first of these, 'The Jew', shows his strong sense of anti-semitism in the Army, which may in turn partly explain his revived interest in Judaism. It was perhaps only when he felt his race and religion were being denigrated that he had any strong urge to defend them. Having turned back to his racial mythology he found that it was rich in themes closely related to his own experiences, as 'The Burning of the Temple' shows (see p. 58).

Rosenberg uses the destruction of Jerusalem by the Babylonian hordes again, in a poem of that title (pp. 57-58), to illustrate the carnage around him:

> Sweet laughter charred in the flame
> That clutched the cloud and earth,
> While Solomon's towers crashed between
> The gird of Babylon's mirth.

He seems to have found comfort, nevertheless, in the thought of his race's survival of a long history of persecution. For he uses it, in 'Through These Pale Cold Days', to suggest that the present catastrophe can also be lived through. It is ironic that the lines were written only a few days before his own death:

> Through these pale cold days
> What dark faces burn
> Out of three thousand years,
> And their wild eyes yearn,

While underneath their brows
Like waifs their spirits grope
For the pools of Hebron again
For Lebanon's summer slope.

They leave these blond still days
In dust behind their tread
They see with living eyes
How long they have been dead.

(pp. 56-57)

Rosenberg's identification with his own race is obvious, yet he felt sufficiently neutral about religion to design a Christmas card for his Division in December 1917, with a suitably Christian verse to accompany it.

In spite of this apparent neutrality Rosenberg applied for a transfer to the Jewish Battalion in Mesopotamia shortly after this verse was written. On the whole his experience in the army seems to have strengthened his pride in his Jewish heritage.

Another significant way in which army life affected Rosenberg was that it forced him to concentrate his creative energies on poetry. Unsuitable conditions and lack of equipment made painting virtually impossible in an army camp and it was out of the question in the trenches. However difficult it was to find the time to write poetry, he was at least able to compose his poems in his head and jot them down in pencil on any available scrap of paper. And in any case, by the time Rosenberg joined the army in late 1915 he had begun to believe in himself 'more as a poet than a painter'. After nearly a year as a soldier he was convinced that he was 'more deep and true as a poet than a painter'.[15] He planned to teach drawing at a school a few days a week when he returned to civilian life, but only because this would leave him, he hoped, 'plenty of leisure to write'.[16] Rosenberg was undoubtedly correct in his choice, for he shows more originality as a poet than painter. Yet part of his originality as a poet stems from his experience as a painter and the two cannot be separated. There is a strong visual element in his poetry which helps to give it a unique quality. Even if we did not know that Rosenberg had sketched the troop-ship and louse-hunting, it would be quite clear from his poems on these two subjects that he had looked at his material with the painter's as well as the poet's vision. Phrases such as 'Grotesque and queerly huddled / Contortionists' and 'Nudes — stark and glistening' compel the reader to visualize the scene in a way which makes it more vivid. We *see* the upturned faces of the soldiers as they look for the larks in one of Rosenberg's most famous poems, 'Returning, We Hear the Larks' (pp. 48-49). We take in the colours of the rat, grey-brown as the trenches, contrasting starkly with the red poppy plucked by the narrator and the 'sleeping green' of no-man's-land in 'Break of Day in the Trenches' (pp. 42-43). Even the last words of this poem — 'Just a little white with the dust' — with their allusion to Man's mortality, are pictorially evocative. Even more powerfully we are made to visualize the horrific scenes in Rosenberg's most ambitious war poem, 'Dead Man's Dump', from its very first lines:

> The plunging limbers over the shattered track
> Racketed with their rusty freight,
> Stuck out like many crowns of thorns,

And the rusty stakes like sceptres old
To stay the flood of brutish men
Upon our brothers dear.
(p. 49)

Sounds too — the 'crunch' of the dead men's bones as
the carriage wheels 'lurch' over them, the 'moans' they
can no longer utter and the shells that 'go crying' over
them — also add weight to the sharply realized visual
details in this poem to conjure up, in broken, disjointed
rhythms, the horrendous scene of carnage.

The visual element in 'Dead Man's Dump' is not only
pronounced, it is also unmistakably Rosenberg's in its
odd, changing angle of vision. The reader views the
scene first through the eyes of 'someone carrying wire
up the line on limbers and running over dead bodies'
(Rosenberg told Marsh), but then through the upturned,
haunted eyes of a dying man waiting for rescue and
finally from the limber-driver's perspective again. The
view from the dying soldier's eyes is particularly disturb-
ing. It is the wagon wheels, the mules' hooves and
quivering bellies we see from ground level upwards. The
normal view of things has been, literally, distorted. This
distortion may be the result of a conscious choice on
Rosenberg's part. That is, it may be a deliberate reject-
ion of straightforward representation in favour of select-
ion of the most significant aspects of the scene, the
verbal equivalent of the Post-Impressionists' technique
which he had already admired and emulated in his paint-
ing. 'Dead Man's Dump' achieves in words what Stanley
Spencer's Burghclere murals, for example, attempt to
capture in paint.

Deliberate or not, Rosenberg's angle of vision is rarely

predictable. Take, for example, 'Louse Hunting' (pp. 47-48). It is only when we know that this is a poem written during the war that we begin to make a connection between the frenzy of the naked men expending so much energy on so unworthy an object as a louse and the soldiers fighting for so dubious a cause. A linking factor is the grotesqueness of the scene. With his painter's eye Rosenberg picks out the most lurid aspects of a scene he has obviously witnessed and relates these indirectly to the obscenity of war.

The connection between the grotesque and war is made more explicit in 'Daughters of War', which Rosenberg thought his best trench poem. 'It has taken me about a year to write', he told Marsh in 1917; 'for I have changed and rechanged it and thought hard over that poem and striven to get that sense of inexorableness the human (or unhuman) side of this war has'.[17] The huge capering figures of his Amazons certainly convey Rosenberg's sense of the awful powers at work in war:

> I saw in prophetic gleams
> These mighty daughters in their dances
> Beckon each soul aghast from its crimson
>   corpse
> To mix in their glittering dances. . .
> (p. 52)

In the second half of the poem Rosenberg claims he has 'penetrated behind human life', for the Amazon who speaks there 'is imagined to be without her lover yet, while all her sisters have theirs, the released spirits of the slain earth men'. By such an ending he hopes to suggest 'the severance of all human relationship and the fading away of human love'.[18]

Like the majority of the trench poems 'Daughters of War' has flaws. Not least of these, as Marsh points out, is its obscurity. Replying to Marsh's criticism, Rosenberg indicates the probable causes of this obscurity, while at the same time explaining his poetic aims in 1917:

> I think with you that poetry should be definite thought and clear expression, however subtle; I don't think there should be any vagueness at all; but a sense of something hidden and felt to be there; now when my things fail to be clear I am sure it is because of the luckless choice of a word or the failure to introduce a word that would flash my idea plain as it is to my own mind.[19]

This rather surprising admission of the possibility of a 'luckless choice of a word' suggests that Rosenberg is not primarily concerned with aesthetic effect. In fact at times he appears almost to glory in the unaesthetic; at other times he seems merely unaware of his clumsiness.

The final stanza of 'In War' (p. 46) reveals another tendency in Rosenberg which sometimes mars, but, curiously enough, often makes his poems:

> What are the great sceptred dooms
> To us, caught
> In the wild wave?
> We break ourselves on them,
> My brother, our hearts and years.

At a first reading the imagery here seems confused to the

point of obscurity, especially in its combining of concrete and abstract — 'sceptred dooms', 'we break ourselves on them . . . our hearts and years'. Then there are so many images packed into one short stanza — sceptres, dooms, wild waves, broken hearts and years. Yet from this very welter of partially, if at all, developed images there emerges a powerful sense of the unbearable grief brought about by Fate. How 'great sceptred dooms' relate to 'the wild wave' we do not know exactly, nor do we care: both images have become symbolic of the violent and merciless, yet majestic nature of war. And it is often the case in other poems of this period. However carelessly they seem (and probably are, at times) thrown together they have an undeniable impact, which perhaps results from that very abandon. 'Break of Day in the Trenches' opens with six lines, in which image is piled upon apparently unrelated image — to symbolic effect:

> The darkness crumbles away —
> It is the same old druid Time as ever.
> Only a live thing leaps my hand —
> A queer sardonic rat —
> As I pull the parapet's poppy
> To stick behind my ear.
> (p. 42)

It is not until we have read the whole poem several times that the symbolism behind these images begins to emerge, yet the initial impact is probably the greater. The three-fold significance of the poppy — its beauty, relating to the lives of the young men, its redness, relating to their spilt blood and its opiate qualities, relating to their probably imminent deaths – is juxtaposed to the ugly but neutral and alive rat. When the poet concludes,

> Poppies whose roots are in man's veins
> Drop, and are ever dropping;
> But mine in my ear is safe,
> Just a little white with the dust,
> (p. 43)

he is undoudtedly referring to his own survival and its precariousness is symbolized by the dust, to which all human beings eventually turn.

In 'Dead Man's Dump' (pp. 49-52) the imagery is more unified than usual and Rosenberg's predictable lack of smoothness is more apparent in the rhythms, which are deliberately harsh and jerky to reflect both the physical progress of the wagons over the corpses and the underlying theme of brutally sudden death. But as the same poem shows, Rosenberg is not incapable of smoothness when it seems to him appropriate:

> None saw their spirits' shadow shake the grass,
> Or stood aside for the half used life to pass
> Out of those doomed nostrils and the
>   doomed mouth,
> When the swift iron burning bee
> Drained the wild honey of their youth.
> (p. 50)

On the whole, however, Rosenberg seems to find harsher rhythms more in keeping with his subject. In 'Returning, We Hear the Larks', for instance, where the title leads us to expect a lyric treatment, he bombards us – in the first half at least — with line after line of strong beats and abrupt rhythms, which suggest the heaviness of the soldiers' spirits as well as their boots:

> Sombre the night is.
> And though we have our lives, we know
> What sinister threat lurks there.
>
> Dragging these anguished limbs, we only
>   know
> This poison-blasted track opens on our
>   camp—
> On a little safe sleep.
>
> (p. 48)

The third stanza is lighter in its rhythms, to reflect the delight felt by the soldiers at the sound of the larks' song:

> But hark! joy—joy—strange joy.
> Lo! heights of night ringing with unseen
>   larks.
> Music showering on our upturned
>   list'ning faces.
>
> (p. 49)

But as the imagery of the final stanza goes on to suggest, there is an underlying irony in the situation which makes the lyric technique seem a deliberate mockery:

> Death could drop from the dark
> As easily as song—
> But song only dropped,
> Like a blind man's dreams on the sand

By dangerous tides,
Like a girl's dark hair for she dreams
    no ruin lies there,
Or her kisses where a serpent hides.
                    (p. 49)
Apart from the skilfulness of its rhythms, 'Returning,
We Hear the Larks' shows that in at least one of his
trench poems Rosenberg achieves mastery of form. The
subject matter is developed through the imagery and
rhythms to a point of resolution where the narrator
accepts the situation and rejoices in the face of all his
fears. It is one of Rosenberg's most perfect poems.

When we consider the poetry of this last period in the
context of Rosenberg's whole output it is important to
remember the conditions under which it was written.
While recognizing that ideally the poet should 'wait on
ideas, (you cannot coax real ones to you) and let as it
were a skin grow naturally round and through them', he
is forced through circumstances 'when the ideas come
hot' to 'seize them with the skin in tatters, raw, crude,
in some parts beautiful in others monstrous'.[20] He him-
self was convinced that going into the army had retard-
ed his development as a poet:

As to what you say about my being luckier than
other victims [he wrote to Schiff] I can only say that
one's individual situation is more real and important
to oneself than the devastations of fates and empires
especially when they do not vitally affect oneself. I
can only give my personal and if you like selfish point
of view that I feeling myself in the prime and vigour
of my powers (whatever they may be) have no more

free will than a tree; seeing with helpless clear eyes the utter destruction of the railways and avenues of approaches to outer communication cut off. Being by the nature of my upbringing, all my energies having been directed to one channel of activity, crippled from other activities and made helpless even to live. It is true I have not been killed or crippled, been a loser in the stocks, or had to forswear my fatherland, but I have not quite gone free and have a right to say something.[21]

It could equally well be argued, however, that the war made Rosenberg as a poet. In the appalling conditions on the Western Front he rejects the last vestiges of Romanticism still evident in his poetry as late as mid-1915. The harshness and horror of his own and others' existence undoubtedly focusses his perception and gives his work an immediacy and edge it previously lacked. His keen eye for visual detail, especially the grotesque, and his detached, almost impersonal attitude now show to their full advantage. His subject matter at last lends itself to his somewhat chaotic method of composition, where image is hurled upon image, the rhythms are highly irregular and the form organic, springing from the material itself. All that is best in his technique comes to fruition in these final poems.

Looking back, his earlier work can be seen as a groping but consistent preparation for the trench poems. The earliest Romantic and Pre-Raphaelite imitations show awkwardnesses which suggest that Rosenberg finds the mode unsuited or inadequate to his needs. While the poems of the middle period, with their experiments in free verse and wider variety of subject matter, indicate a more conscious rejection of a smooth technique. He now finds this inappropriate to the harsh vision he is at last beginning to realise, but which is not fully expressed until the trench poems.

It is interesting to consider the possible course of Rosenberg's poetry had he lived. We have some indication of this in the poem he was working on at his death. 'The Unicorn', as this dramatic fragment came to be called, suggests that he was not satisfied with the mainly lyric form of his previous works. He had already shown a desire to produce something weightier in 'Moses', both plays being an attempt to symbolize the war in epic terms. Less than a month before he died he wrote to Miss Seaton: 'If I am lucky, and come off undamaged, I mean to put all my innermost experiences into the "Unicorn". I want it to symbolize the war and all the devastating forces let loose by an unscrupulous will'.[22] He had been working consistently on 'The Unicorn' for nearly a year when he wrote this letter, but its genesis went back as far as mid-1916 with the composition of a fragment called 'The Amulet'. This deals with the three main characters in 'The Unicorn' — Saul, Lilith and the Nubian (later called Tel). The Nubian's power over Lilith, whom he desires, is symbolized by his green jade amulet. As he worked on the play, however, Rosenberg discarded this symbol in favour of another more powerful one — the unicorn. Its phallic overtones were more appropriate to his revised intention, which he explained to Edward Marsh in mid-1917:

Its a kind of 'Rape of the Sabine Women', idea. Some

strange race of wanderers have settled in some wild strange place and are perishing out for lack of women. The prince of these explores some country near where the women are most fair. But the natives will not hear of foreign marriages; and he plots another rape of the Sabines, but he is trapped in the act.

Another variation Rosenberg contemplated was to have the story of the decaying race told in a myth which was to be read by Lilith, the wife of Saul. 'Saul and Lilith', he told Marsh, 'are ordinary folks into whose ordinary lives the Unicorn bursts. It is to be a play of terror—terror of hidden things and the fear of the supernatural'. Though he abandoned the idea of Lilith reading the myth, in favour of her being actually confronted by Tel and his race, Rosenberg kept the theme of terror, which gave rise to one of the most powerful passages in the last version he sent to Gordon Bottomley a few days before his death. Here Lilith's fear and Tel's sense of his race's imminent extinction is brought out through that grotesque and striking imagery verging on symbolism, which Rosenberg had mastered in his war poetry:

TEL. By now my men have raided the city,
 I heard a far shrieking.
LILITH. This is most piteous, most fearful,
 I fear him, his hungry eyes
 Burn into me, like those balls of fire.
TEL. There is a tower of skulls,
 Where birds make nests
 And staring beasts stand by with many flocks

And man looks on with hopeless eyes ...
LILITH. O horrible, I hear Saul rattle those chains in
the cellar.
TEL. What clanking chains?
When a man's brains crack with longing
We chain him to some slender beast to breed.

The conclusion, which immediately follows this passage,
shows a much stronger sense of form than any previous
work of comparable length. As Saul, Lilith and her
cousin's husband Enoch confront Tel, his dying race
ride past the window:

> . . . *a black naked host on various animals, the
> Unicorn leading. A woman is clasped on every one,
> some are frantic, others white or unconscious, some
> nestle laughing.* ENOCH *with madness in his eyes leaps
> through the casement and disappears with a splash in
> the well.* SAUL *leaps after him shouting 'The Unicorn'.*
> TEL *places* LILITH *on the Unicorn and they all ride
> away.*

However crude Rosenberg's attempt to round off his
play, it promises a greater control of form than in his
earlier work. At the age of twenty-seven he was, as he
says, in 'the prime and vigour of [his] powers', though
he was not given time fully to demonstrate these.
Though singularly lacking in irony himself his death was
highly ironic, for he survived almost two years under the
most appalling conditions, only to be killed on April
Fools' Day seven months before the end of the war.

J.M.W.

Notes

1. *The Collected Works of Isaac Rosenberg*, ed. Ian Parsons (Chatto & Windus, 1984), p. ix.
2. Letter to Miss Winifreda Seaton (whom Rosenberg had met at his friend and neighbour, J.H.Amschewitz's studio in 1910), n.d., *Collected Works*, p. 180.
3. ibid., pp. 180-81.
4. ibid., p. 181.
5. [late December 1915], ibid., p. 227.
6. ibid.
7. Rosenberg to Mrs Cohen, n.d., ibid., p. 237.
8. ibid., p. 248.
9. ibid.
10. ibid., p. 278.
11. ibid., p. 287.
12. *Journey to the Trenches* (Robson Books, 1975), p. 140.
13. *Collected Works*, p. 248.
14. [March 1918], ibid., p. 270.
15. Rosenberg to Sydney Schiff, [late July 1916], ibid., p. 239.
16. ibid.
17. Rosenberg to Edward Marsh, [postmarked 30 July 1917], ibid., p. 260.
18. [June 1917], ibid., p. 257.
19. [postmarked 30 July 1917], ibid., p. 260.
20. Rosenberg to Marsh, 4 August [1916], ibid., p. 239.
21. [October 1915], ibid., p. 218.
22. Rosenberg to Miss Seaton, [8 March 1918], ibid., p. 270.

The War Years

On Receiving News of
the War

Snow is a strange white word;
No ice or frost
Has asked of bud or bird
For Winter's cost.

Yet ice and frost and snow
From earth to sky
This Summer land doth know;
No man knows why.

In all men's hearts it is;
Some spirit old
Hath turned with malign kiss
Our lives to mould.

Red fangs have torn His face,
God's blood is shed:
He mourns from His lone place
His children dead.

O ancient crimson curse!
Corrode, consume;
Give back this universe
Its pristine bloom.

Cape Town 1914

The Dead Heroes

Flame out, you glorious skies,
Welcome our brave;
Kiss their exultant eyes;
Give what they gave.

Flash, mailèd seraphim,
Your burning spears;
New days to outflame their dim
Heroic years.

Thrills their baptismal tread
The bright proud air;
The embattled plumes outspread
Burn upwards there.

Flame out, flame out, O Song!
Star ring to star;
Strong as our hurt is strong
Our children are.

Their blood is England's heart;
By their dead hands
It is their noble part
That England stands.

England—Time gave them thee;
They gave back this
To win Eternity
And claim God's kiss.

Marching

(As Seen from the Left File)

My eyes catch ruddy necks
Sturdily pressed back—
All a red-brick moving glint.
Like flaming pendulums, hands
Swing across the khaki—
Mustard-coloured khaki—
To the automatic feet.

We husband the ancient glory
In these bared necks and hands.
Not broke is the forge of Mars;
But a subtler brain beats iron
To shoe the hoofs of death
(Who paws dynamic air now).
Blind fingers loose an iron cloud
To rain immortal darkness
On strong eyes.

August 1914

What in our lives is burnt
In the fire of this?
The heart's dear granary?
The much we shall miss?

Three lives hath one life—
Iron, honey, gold.
The gold, the honey gone—
Left is the hard and cold.

Iron are our lives
Molten right through our youth.
A burnt space through ripe fields
A fair mouth's broken tooth.

The Troop Ship

Grotesque and queerly huddled
Contortionists to twist
The sleepy soul to a sleep,
We lie all sorts of ways
And cannot sleep.
The wet wind is so cold,
And the lurching men so careless,
That, should you drop to a doze,
Winds' fumble or men's feet
Are on your face.

From France

The spirit drank the café lights;
All the hot life that glittered there,
And heard men say to women gay,
'Life is just so in France'.

The spirit dreams of café lights,
And golden faces and soft tones,
And hears men groan to broken men,
'This is not Life in France'.

Heaped stones and a charred signboard show
With grass between and dead folk under,
And some birds sing, while the spirit takes wing.
And this is Life in France.

Spring, 1916

Slow, rigid, is this masquerade
That passes as through a difficult air;
Heavily—heavily passes.
What has she fed on? Who her table laid
Through the three seasons? What forbidden fare
Ruined her as a mortal lass is?

I played with her two years ago,
Who might be now her own sister in stone;
So altered from her May mien,

When round the pink a necklace of warm snow
Laughed at her throat where my mouth's touch had gone.
How is this, ruined Queen?

Who lured her vivid beauty so
To be that strained chill thing that moves
So ghastly midst her young brood
Of pregnant shoots that she for men did grow?
Where are the strong men who made these their loves?
Spring! God pity your mood!

Break of Day in the Trenches

The darkness crumbles away—
It is the same old druid Time as ever.
Only a live thing leaps my hand—
A queer sardonic rat—
As I pull the parapet's poppy
To stick behind my ear.
Droll rat, they would shoot you if they knew
Your cosmopolitan sympathies
(And God knows what antipathies).
Now you have touched this English hand
You will do the same to a German—
Soon, no doubt, if it be your pleasure
To cross the sleeping green between.
It seems you inwardly grin as you pass
Strong eyes, fine limbs, haughty athletes
Less chanced than you for life;
Bonds to the whims of murder,

Sprawled in the bowels of the earth,
The torn fields of France.
What do you see in our eyes
At the shrieking iron and flame
Hurled through still heavens?
What quaver—what heart aghast?
Poppies whose roots are in man's veins
Drop, and are ever dropping;
But mine in my ear is safe,
Just a little white with the dust.

Home Thoughts from France

Wan, fragile faces of joy,
Pitiful mouths that strive
To light with smiles the place
We dream we walk alive,

To you I stretch my hands,
Hands shut in pitiless trance
In a land of ruin and woe,
The desolate land of France.

Dear faces startled and shaken,
Out of wild dust and sounds
You yearn to me, lure and sadden
My heart with futile bounds.

The Dying Soldier

'Here are the houses,' he moaned,
'I could reach, but my brain swims.'
Then they thundered and flashed,
And shook the earth to its rims.

'They are gunpits,' he gasped,
'Our men are at the guns.
Water! . . . Water! . . . Oh, water!
For one of England's dying sons.'

'We cannot give you water,
Were all England in your breath.'
'Water! . . . Water! . . . Oh, water!'
He moaned and swooned to death.

In War

Fret the nonchalant noon
With your spleen
Or your gay brow,
For the motion of your spirit
Ever moves with these.

When day shall be too quiet,
Deaf to you
And your dumb smile,
Untuned air shall lap the stillness
In the old space for your voice —

The voice that once could mirror
Remote depths
Of moving being,
Stirred by responsive voices near,
Suddenly stilled for ever.

No ghost darkens the places
Dark to One;
But my eyes dream,
And my heart is heavy to think
How it was heavy once.

In the old days when death
Stalked the world
For the flower of men,
And the rose of beauty faded
And pined in the great gloom,

One day we dug a grave:
We were vexed
With the sun's heat.
We scanned the hooded dead:
At noon we sat and talked.

How death had kissed their eyes
Three dread noons since,
How human art won
The dark soul to flicker
Till it was lost again:

And we whom chance kept whole—
But haggard,

Spent—were charged
To make a place for them who knew
No pain in any place.

The good priest came to pray;
Our ears half heard,
And half we thought
Of alien things, irrelevant;
And the heat and thirst were great.

The good priest read: 'I heard . . . '
Dimly my brain
Held words and lost. . . .
Sudden my blood ran cold. . . .
God! God! It could not be.

He read my brother's name;
I sank—
I clutched the priest.
They did not tell me it was he
Was killed three days ago.

What are the great sceptred dooms
To us, caught
In the wild wave?
We break ourselves on them,
My brother, our hearts and years.

The Immortals

I killed them, but they would not die.
Yea, all the day and all the night
For them I could not rest nor sleep,
Nor guard from them nor hide in flight!

Then in my agony I turned
And made my hands red in their gore.
In vain — for faster than I slew
They rose more cruel than before.

I killed and killed with slaughter mad;
I killed till all my strength was gone;
And still they rose to torture me,
For Devils only die for fun.

I used to think the Devil hid
In women's smiles and wine's carouse;
I called him Satan, Balzebub;
But now I call him dirty louse.

Louse Hunting

Nudes, stark and glistening,
Yelling in lurid glee. Grinning faces
And raging limbs
Whirl over the floor one fire;
For a shirt verminously busy
Yon soldier tore from his throat

With oaths
Godhead might shrink at, but not the lice,
And soon the shirt was aflare
Over the candle he'd lit while we lay.

Then we all sprang up and stript
To hunt the verminous brood.
Soon like a demons' pantomime
This plunge was raging.
See the silhouettes agape,
See the gibbering shadows
Mixed with the baffled arms on the wall.
See Gargantuan hooked fingers
Pluck in supreme flesh
To smutch supreme littleness.
See the merry limbs in that Highland fling
Because some wizard vermin willed
To charm from the quiet this revel
When our ears were half lulled
By the dark music
Blown from Sleep's trumpet.

Returning, We Hear the Larks

Sombre the night is:
And, though we have our lives, we know
What sinister threat lurks there.

Dragging these anguished limbs, we only know
This poison-blasted track opens on our camp —
On a little safe sleep.

But hark! Joy—joy—strange joy.
Lo! Heights of night ringing with unseen larks:
Music showering on our upturned listening faces.

Death could drop from the dark
As easily as song—
But song only dropped,
Like a blind man's dreams on the sand
By dangerous tides;
Like a girl's dark hair, for she dreams no ruin lies there,
Or her kisses where a serpent hides.

Dead Man's Dump

The plunging limbers over the shattered track
Racketed with their rusty freight,
Stuck out like many crowns of thorns,
And the rusty stakes like sceptres old
To stay the flood of brutish men
Upon our brothers dear.

The wheels lurched over sprawled dead
But pained them not, though their bones crunched;
Their shut mouths made no moan.
They lie there huddled, friend and foeman,
Man born of man, and born of woman;
And shells go crying over them
From night till night and now.

Earth has waited for them,

All the time of their growth
Fretting for their decay:
Now she has them at last!
In the strength of their strength
Suspended—stopped and held.

What fierce imaginings their dark souls lit?
Earth! Have they gone into you?
Somewhere they must have gone,
And flung on your hard back
Is their souls' sack,
Emptied of God-ancestralled essences.
Who hurled them out? Who hurled?

None saw their spirits' shadow shake the grass,
Or stood aside for the half used life to pass
Out of those doomed nostrils and the doomed mouth,
When the swift iron burning bee
Drained the wild honey of their youth.

What of us who, flung on the shrieking pyre,
Walk, our usual thoughts untouched,
Our lucky limbs as on ichor fed,
Immortal seeming ever?
Perhaps when the flames beat loud on us,
A fear may choke in our veins
And the startled blood may stop.

The air is loud with death,
The dark air spurts with fire,
The explosions ceaseless are.
Timelessly now, some minutes past,

These dead strode time with vigorous life,
Till the shrapnell called 'An end!'
But not to all. In bleeding pangs
Some borne on stretchers dreamed of home,
Dear things, war-blotted from their hearts.

A man's brains splattered on
A stretcher-bearer's face;
His shook shoulders slipped their load,
But when they bent to look again
The drowning soul was sunk too deep
For human tenderness.

They left this dead with the older dead,
Stretched at the cross roads.

Burnt black by strange decay
Their sinister faces lie,
The lid over each eye;
The grass and coloured clay
More motion have than they,
Joined to the great sunk silences.

Here is one not long dead.
His dark hearing caught our far wheels,
And the choked soul stretched weak hands
To reach the living word the far wheels said;
The blood-dazed intelligence beating for light,
Crying through the suspense of the far torturing wheels
Swift for the end to break,
Or the wheels to break,
Cried as the tide of the world broke over his sight,

'Will they come? Will they ever come?'
Even as the mixed hoofs of the mules,
The quivering-bellied mules,
And the rushing wheels all mixed
With his tortured upturned sight.
So we crashed round the bend,
We heard his weak scream,
We heard his very last sound,
And our wheels grazed his dead face.

Daughters of War

Space beats the ruddy freedom of their limbs,
Their naked dances with man's spirit naked
By the root side of the tree of life
(The under side of things
And shut from earth's profoundest eyes).

I saw in prophetic gleams
These mighty daughters in their dances
Beckon each soul aghast from its crimson corpse
To mix in their glittering dances:
I heard the mighty daughters' giant sighs
In sleepless passion for the sons of valour
And envy of the days of flesh,
Barring their love with mortal boughs across—
The mortal boughs, the mortal tree of life.
The old bark burnt with iron wars
They blow to a live flame

To char the young green days
And reach the occult soul; they have no softer lure,
No softer lure than the savage ways of death.
We were satisfied of our lords the moon and the sun
To take our wage of sleep and bread and warmth —
These maidens came — these strong everliving Amazons,
And in an easy might their wrists
Of night's sway and noon's sway the sceptres brake,
Clouding the wild, the soft lustres of our eyes.

Clouding the wild lustres, the clinging tender lights;
Driving the darkness into the flame of day
With the Amazonian wind of them
Over our corroding faces
That must be broken — broken for evermore,
So the soul can leap out
Into their huge embraces.
Though there are human faces
Best sculptures of Deity,
And sinews lusted after
By the Archangels tall,
Even these must leap to the love-heat of these maidens
From the flame of terrene days,
Leaving grey ashes to the wind — to the wind.

One (whose great lifted face,
Where wisdom's strength and beauty's strength
And the thewed strength of large beasts
Moved and merged, gloomed and lit)
Was speaking, surely, as the earth-men's earth fell away;
Whose new hearing drank the sound
Where pictures, lutes, and mountains mixed

With the loosed spirit of a thought,
Essenced to language thus —

'My sisters force their males
From the doomed earth, from the doomed glee
And hankering of hearts.
Frail hands gleam up through the human quagmire,
    and lips of ash
Seem to wail, as in sad faded paintings
Far-sunken and strange.
My sisters have their males
Clean of the dust of old days
That clings about those white hands
And yearns in those voices sad:
But these shall not see them,
Or think of them in any days or years;
They are my sisters' lovers in other days and years.'

Soldier: Twentieth Century

I love you, great new Titan!
Am I not you?
Napoleon and Caesar
Out of you grew.

Out of unthinkable torture,
Eyes kissed by death,
Won back to the world again,
Lost and won in a breath,

Cruel men are made immortal.
Out of your pain born,
They have stolen the sun's power
With their feet on your shoulders worn.

Let them shrink from your girth,
That has outgrown the pallid days
When you slept like Circe's swine
Or a word in the brain's ways.

Girl to Soldier on Leave

I love you, Titan lover,
My own storm-days' Titan.
Greater than the son of Zeus,
I know whom I would choose.

Titan — my splendid rebel —
The old Prometheus
Wanes like a ghost before your power:
His pangs were joys to yours.

Pallid days, arid and wan,
Tied your soul fast:
Babel-cities' smoky tops
Pressed upon your growth

Weary gyves. What were you
But a word in the brain's ways,

Or the sleep of Circe's swine?
One gyve holds you yet.

It held you hiddenly on the Somme
Tied from my heart at home:
O must it loosen now? I wish
You were bound with the old, old gyves.

Love! You love me—your eyes
Have looked through death at mine.
You have tempted a grave too much.
I let you—I repine.

The Jew

Moses, from whose loins I sprung,
Lit by a lamp in his blood
Ten immutable rules, a moon
For mutable lampless men.

The blonde, the bronze, the ruddy,
With the same heaving blood,
Keep tide to the moon of Moses.
Then why do they sneer at me?

'Through these Pale Cold Days'

Through these pale cold days
What dark faces burn
Out of three thousand years,

And their wild eyes yearn,

While underneath their brows
Like waifs their spirits grope
For the pools of Hebron again —
For Lebanon's summer slope.

They leave these blond still days
In dust behind their tread
They see with living eyes
How long they have been dead.

The Destruction of Jerusalem by the Babylonian Hordes

They left their Babylon bare
Of all its tall men,
Of all its proud horses;
They made for Lebanon.

And shadowy sowers went
Before their spears to sow
The fruit whose taste is ash,
For Judah's soul to know.

They who bowed to the Bull god,
Whose wings roofed Babylon,
In endless hosts darkened
The bright-heavened Lebanon.

They washed their grime in pools
Where laughing girls forgot
The wiles they used for Solomon.
Sweet laughter, remembered not!

Sweet laughter charred in the flame
That clutched the cloud and earth,
While Solomon's towers crashed between
To a gird of Babylon's mirth.

The Burning of the Temple

Fierce wrath of Solomon,
Where sleepest thou? O see,
The fabric which thou won
Earth and ocean to give thee—
O look at the red skies.

Or hath the sun plunged down?
What is this molten gold—
These thundering fires blown
Through heaven, where the smoke rolled?
Again the great king dies.

His dreams go out in smoke.
His days he let not pass
And sculptured here are broke,
Are charred as the burnt grass,
Gone as his mouth's last sighs.

Earlier Poems

Zion

She stood — a hill-ensceptred Queen,
   The glory streaming from her;
While Heaven flashed her rays between,
   And shed eternal summer.

The gates of morning opened wide
   On sunny dome and steeple;
Noon gleamed upon the mountain-side
   Thronged with a happy people;

And twilight's drowsy, half closed eyes
   Beheld that virgin splendour
Whose orbs were as her darkening skies,
   And as her spirit, tender.

Girt with that strength, first-born of right,
   Held fast by deeds of honour,
Her robe she wove with rays more bright
   Than Heaven could rain upon her.

Where is that light — that citadel?
   That robe with woof of glory?
She lost her virtue and she fell,
   And only left her story.

1906; written at the age of sixteen.

A Ballad of Whitechapel

God's mercy shines;
And our full hearts must make record of this,
For grief that burst from out its dark confines
Into strange sunlit bliss.

I stood where glowed
The merry glare of golden whirring lights
Above the monstrous mass that seethed and flowed
Through one of London's nights.

I watched the gleams
Of jaggèd warm lights on shrunk faces pale:
I heard mad laughter as one hears in dreams
Or Hell's harsh lurid tale.

The traffic rolled,
A gliding chaos populous of din,
A steaming wail at doom the Lord had scrawled
For perilous loads of sin.

And my soul thought:
'What fearful land have my steps wandered to?
God's love is everywhere, but here is naught
Save love His anger slew.'

And as I stood
Lost in promiscuous bewilderment,
Which to my mazèd soul was wonder-food,
A girl in garments rent

Peered 'neath lids shamed
And spoke to me and murmured to my blood.
My soul stopped dead, and all my horror flamed
At her forgot of God.

Her hungered eyes,
Craving and yet so sadly spiritual,
Shone like the unsmirched corner of a jewel
Where else foul blemish lies.

I walked with her
Because my heart thought, 'Here the soul is clean,
The fragrance of the frankincense and myrrh
Is lost in odours mean.'

She told me how
The shadow of black death had newly come
And touched her father, mother, even now
Grim-hovering in her home,

Where fevered lay
Her wasting brother in a cold, bleak room,
Which theirs would be no longer than a day,
And then—the streets and doom.

Lord! Lord! Dear Lord!
I knew that life was bitter, but my soul
Recoiled, as anguish-smitten by sharp sword,
Grieving such body's dole.

Then grief gave place
To a strange pulsing rapture as she spoke;

For I could catch the glimpses of God's grace,
And a desire awoke

To take this trust
And warm and gladden it with love's new fires,
Burning the past to ashes and to dust
Through purified desires.

We walked our way,
One way hewn for us from the birth of Time;
For we had wandered into Love's strange clime
Through ways sin waits to slay.

Love's euphony,
In Love's own temple that is our glad hearts,
Makes now long music wild deliciously;
Now Grief hath used his darts.

Love infinite,
Chastened by sorrow, hallowed by pure flame —
Not all the surging world can compass it.
Love — Love — O tremulous name!

God's mercy shines;
And my full heart hath made record of this,
Of grief that burst from out its dark confines
Into strange sunlit bliss.

1910

My Days

My days are but the tombs of buried hours;
Which tombs are hidden in the pilèd years;
But from the mounds there spring up many flowers,
Whose beauty well repays their cost of tears.
Time, like a sexton, pileth mould on mould,
Minutes on minutes till the tombs are high;
But from the dust there fall some grains of gold,
And the dead corpse leaves what will never die—
It may be but a thought, the nursling seed
Of many thoughts, of many a high desire;
Some little act that stirs a noble deed,
Like breath rekindling a smouldering fire:
They only live who have not lived in vain,
For in their works their life returns again.

1911

Spiritual Isolation: a Fragment

My Maker shunneth me;
Even as a wretch stricken with leprosy
So hold I pestilent supremacy.
Yea! He hath fled far as the uttermost star,
Beyond the unperturbed fastnesses of night
And dreams that bastioned are
By fretted towers of sleep that scare His light.

Of wisdom writ, whereto
My burdened feet may haste withouten rue,
I may not spell—and I am sore to do.
Yea, all (seeing my Maker hath such dread),
Even mine own self-love, wists not but to fly
To Him, and sore besped
Leaves me, its captain, in such mutiny.

Will, deemed incorporate
With me, hath flown ere love, to expiate
Its sinful stay where He did habitate.
Ah me, if they had left a sepulchre;
But no—the light hath changed not, and in it
Of its same colour stir
Spirits I see not but phantasmed feel to flit.

Air, legioned with such, stirreth,
So that I seem to draw them with my breath,
Ghouls that devour each joy they do to death,
Strange glimmering griefs and sorrowing silences
Bearing dead flowers unseen whose charnel smell
Great awe to my sense is
Even in the rose-time when all else is well.

*   *   *   *

1911-12

O, in a World of Men and Women

O, in a world of men and women,
Where all things seemed so strange to me,
And speech the common world called human
For me was a vain mimicry,

I thought—O, am I one in sorrow?
Or is the world more quick to hide
Their pain with raiment that they borrow
From pleasure in the house of pride?

O joy of mine, O longed-for stranger,
How I would greet you if you came:
In the world's joys I've been a ranger,
In my world sorrow is their name.

1911-12

The Blind God

Streaked with immortal blasphemies,
Betwixt His twin eternities
The Shaper of mortal destinies
Sits in that limbo of dreamless sleep,
Some nothing that hath shadows deep.

The world is only a small pool
In the meadows of Eternity,

And men like fishes lying cool;
And the wise man and the fool
In its depths like fishes lie.
When an angel drops a rod
And he draws you to the sky
Will you bear to meet your God
You have streaked with blasphemy?

1913

Song

A silver rose to show
Is your sweet face;
And like the heavens' white brow,
Sometime God's battle-place,
Your blood is quiet now.

Your body is a star
Unto my thought;
But stars are not too far,
And can be caught—
Small pools their prisons are.

The Female God

We curl into your eyes—
They drink our fires and have never drained;
In the fierce forest of your hair
Our desires beat blindly for their treasure.

In your eyes' subtle pit,
Far down, glimmer our souls;
And your hair like massive forest trees
Shadows our pulses, overtired and dumb.

Like a candle lost in an electric glare
Our spirits tread your eyes' infinities;
In the wrecking waves of your tumultuous locks
Do you not hear the moaning of our pulses?

Queen! Goddess! Animal!
In sleep do your dreams battle with our souls?
When your hair is spread like a lover on the pillow
Do not our jealous pulses wake between?

You have dethroned the ancient God,
You have usurped his Sabbath, his common days;
Yea, every moment is delivered to you,
Our Temple, our Eternal, our one God!

Our souls have passed into your eyes,
Our days into your hair;

And you, our rose-deaf prison, are very pleased
　　with the world,
Your world.

1914

In the Underworld

I have lived in the underworld so long:
How can you, a creature of light,
Without terror understand the song
And unmoved hear what moves in night?

I am a spirit that yours has found,
Strange, undelightful, obscure,
Created by some other God, and bound
In terrible darkness, breathing breath impure.

Creature of light and happiness,
Deeper the darkness was when you,
With your bright terror eddying the distress,
Grazed the dark waves and shivering further flew.

1914

Wedded

They leave their love-lorn haunts,
Their sigh-warm floating Eden;
And they are mute at once,
Mortals by God unheeden,
By their past kisses chidden.

But they have kist and known
Clear things we dim by guesses—
Spirit to spirit grown:
Heaven, born in hand-caresses—
Love, fall from sheltering tresses.

And they are dumb and strange:
Bared trees bowed from each other.
Their last green interchange
What lost dreams shall discover?
Dead, strayed, to love-strange lover.

Midsummer Frost

A July ghost, aghast at the strange winter,
Wonders, at burning noon (all summer seeming),
How, like a sad thought buried in light words,
Winter, an alien presence, is ambushed here.

See, from the fire-fountained noon, there creep

Lazy yellow ardours towards pale evening,
To thread dark and vain fire
Over my unsens'd heart,
Dead heart, no urgent summer can reach.
Hidden as a root from air or a star from day;
A frozen pool whereon mirth dances;
Where the shining boys would fish.

My blinded brain pierced is,
And searched by a thought, and pangful
With bitter ooze of a joyous knowledge
Of some starred time outworn.
Like blind eyes that have slinked past God,
And light, their untasked inheritance,
(Sealed eyes that trouble never the Sun)
Yet has feel of a Maytime pierced.
He heareth the Maytime dances;
Frees from their airy prison, bright voices,
To loosen them in his dark imagination,

Powered with girl revels rare
And silks and merry colours,
And all the unpeopled ghosts that walk in words.
Till wave white hands that ripple lakes of sadness,
Until the sadness vanishes and the stagnant pool remains.

Underneath this summer air can July dream
How, in night hanging forest of eating maladies,
A frozen forest of moon unquiet madness,
The moon-drunk haunted pierced soul dies;
Starved by its Babel folly, lying stark,
Unvexed by July's warm eyes.

If You Are Fire

If you are fire and I am fire,
Who blows the flame apart
So that desire eludes desire
Around one central heart?

A single root and separate bough,
And what blind hands between
That make our longing's mutual glow
As if it had not been?

The One Lost

I mingle with your bones.
You steal in subtle noose
This lighted dust Jehovah loans
And now I lose.

What will the Lender say
When I shall not be found,
Safe sheltered at the Judgment Day,
Being in you bound?

He'll hunt throng'd wards of Heaven,
Call to uncoffined earth,
'Where is this soul unjudged, not given
Dole for good's dearth?'

And I, lying so safe
Within you, hearing all,
To have cheated God shall laugh,
Freed by your thrall.

'My Soul is Robbed'

My soul is robbed by your most treacherous eyes
Treading its intricate infinities.
Stay there, rich robbers! what I lose is dross;
Since my life is your dungeon, where is loss?

Ah! as the sun is prisoned in the heaven,
Whose walls dissolve, of their own nature bereaven,
So do your looks, as idly, without strife,
Cover all steeps of sense, which no more pasture life.
Which no more feel, but only know you there,
In this blind trance of some white anywhere.

Come—come—that glance engendered ecstasy—
That subtle unspaced mutual intimacy
Whereby two spirits of one thought commune
Like separate instruments that play one tune,
And the whole miracle and amazement of
The unexpected flowering of love
Concentres to an instant that expands
And takes unto itself the strangest of strange lands.

The Cloister

Our eyes no longer sail the tidal streets,
Nor harbour where the hours like petals float
By sensual treasures glittering through thin walls
Of woman's eyes and colour's mystery.

The roots of our eternal souls were fed
On the world's dung and now their blossoms gleam.
God gives to glisten in an angel's hair
These He has gardened, for they please His eyes.

Expression

Call—call—and bruise the air:
Shatter dumb space!
Yea! We will fling this passion everywhere;
Leaving no place

For the superb and grave
Magnificent throng,
The pregnant queens of quietness that brave
And edge our song

Of wonder at the light
(Our life-leased home),
Of greeting to our housemates.
    And in might
Our song shall roam

Life's heart, a blossoming fire
Blown bright by thought,
While gleams and fades the infinite desire,
Phantasmed naught.

Can this be caught and caged?
Wings can be clipt
Of eagles, the sun's gaudy measure gauged,
But no sense dipt

In the mystery of sense.
The troubled throng
Of words break out like smothered fire through dense
And smouldering wrong.

First Fruit

I did not pluck at all,
And I am sorry now:
The garden is not barred
But the boughs are heavy with snow,
The flake-blossoms thickly fall
And the hid roots sigh, 'How long will
    our flowers be marred?'
Strange as a bird were dumb,
Strange as a hueless leaf.
As one deaf hungers to hear,
Or gazes without belief,
The fruit yearned 'Fingers, come!'
O, shut hands, be empty another year.

Chagrin

Caught still as Absalom,
Surely the air hangs
From the swayless cloud-boughs
Like hair of Absalom
Caught and hanging still.

From the imagined weight
Of spaces in a sky
Of mute chagrin my thoughts
Hang like branch-clung hair
To trunks of silence swung,
With the choked soul weighing down
Into thick emptiness.
Christ, end this hanging death,
For endlessness hangs therefrom!

Invisibly branches break
From invisible trees:
The cloud-woods where we rush
(Our eyes holding so much),
Which we must ride dim ages round
Ere the hands (we dream) can touch,
We ride, we ride—before the morning
The secret roots of the sun to tread—
And suddenly
We are lifted of all we know,
And hang from implacable boughs.

Heart's First Word. II

And all her soft dark hair
Breathed for him like a prayer,
And her white lost face
Was prisoned to some far place.
Love was not denied —
Love's ends would hide,
And flower and fruit and tree
Were under its sea.
Yea, its abundance knelt
Where the nerves felt
The springs of feeling flow
And made pain grow!
There seemed no root or sky,
But a pent infinity
Where apparitions dim
Sculptured each whim
In flame and wandering mist
Of kisses to be kist.

Index of First Lines of Poems